Words to Read in Times of Illness

IRH PRESS

BOOKS
IRH PRESS
New York

ISBN: 978-1-958655-07-8
Cover Image: Maya Kruchankova / shutterstock.com

Printed in Canada

First Edition

Words _to_ Read _in_ Times _of_ Illness

EL CANTARE

Ryuho Okawa

IRH PRESS

Contents

Words to Read in Times of Illness

Words to Read
in Times of Illness

(1)

Times of illness are
days of rest for the soul.

(2)

Recall the memories
you have left behind.

③

Feeling pain means

you are still alive.

In your hospital bed, think of

the joy of having freedom.

$\textcircled{5}$

Reflect on the harmony

between your mind and body.

Remember the people
you have loved in your life.

Think about death that is

steadily approaching.

8

If there is someone that you can

no longer apologize to directly,

sincerely apologize in your heart.

$$\textcircled{9}$$

Be thankful that you have been
given life, now, in this age.

10

Think about how trivial
your pride is in this world.

(11)

Once you realize that your
remaining time is limited,
think about how you will spend
each of the remaining days.

(12)

Think about the people
you know or your friends
who have fallen ill.

Contemplate on the moment

you were brought into this world.

Ponder on the night sky
full of stars.

Be thankful to your body that
continues to eat well, urinate,
and defecate every day.

16

Whether it has been good or bad,

you have a father and a mother

who brought you into this world.

Your life can be traced back

through centuries or

even tens of centuries.

18

Be thankful that

your life began with love.

When you are in a fight with someone, remember that you are still alive. Be thankful for this.

(20)

Forgive others' sins and forget
their hurtful words and actions.

21

If you have been jealous of
someone, accept that you
actually admire their talents.

(22)

Think that society has prospered because there were many people who were more talented than you.

(23)

Be thankful that the opposite sex

exists in this world.

Do you remember

your first love?

(25)

Quietly say,

"Thank you, God,

for giving me life."

Think that even a heartbreak was

a chance for you to grow.

$\widehat{27}$

Try to praise yourself a little for
enduring the physical pain.

Imagine that your body is

a small universe made up of

hundreds of millions of cells.

(29)

When you are ill,

you may lose your beauty and

whether you are a beautiful

woman or a handsome man

becomes less important to you.

30

How wonderful it is

to be alive today as well.

(31)

Be thankful to the many people

who have made you

who you are today.

Was your life like a flower

blooming in a flowerbed?

(33)

Were you able to help improve someone else's life?

If you are a bad son or daughter,

try to own up to it and apologize

to the world.

Say to the sick part of your body,

"Thank you for all your

hard work over the years."

(36)

Reflect on whether your feelings
of hatred, sadness, and pain are
the cause of your ailment.

Once you have recovered,

what are the things you want to do?

Play with your imagination.

(38)

When you have a fever,

think that it means your cells are

trying their best to live.

Shakyamuni Buddha referred to "Birth, Aging, Illness, and Death" as "The Four Pains." You, too, have a chance to be enlightened.

Don't give in to desperation.

God has kept you alive until now—

think of this miracle.

When you are feeling sad about
having less control over your body,
think of the people living in
times of war.

Doctors tend to tell you how bad

your condition is. But just think

that they are saying it because

they care for you.

Don't forget to

smile at nurses and say,

"Thank you for your hard work."

Be thankful to your family
members in your heart,
whether they may visit you
at the hospital or not.

Did you fulfill your own mission as a member of your family?

Reflect on how hard you studied

and played sports as a student

and how much you contributed

to society as an adult.

For the relationships that are
too late to fix, ask for forgiveness
from God or Buddha.

If all this time you have only

been thinking about money,

now, think about the mind.

Whether you have been boastful

about your education or

making it the cause of your misery,

try thinking about other

sick people.

How well did you

take care of your health and fitness

before you got ill?

Give yourself a score.

$$\boxed{51}$$

Because there is death,

there is new life.

Believe in reincarnation.

Some people experience

a great turning point in life

after having an accident.

$$\boxed{53}$$

We have two hands and
can grab hold of things;
even that is happiness.

We have two legs to

stand and walk on.

Be thankful for this miracle.

We can see things with our eyes.
This is something to be thankful
for, even if we need to wear
glasses or contact lenses.

We can breathe on our own

through our nose.

Even if we cannot do so now,

we were once able to.

This is truly a blessing.

We have a mouth and we can eat. Even if we need help from others to eat, isn't it wonderful?

Our teeth come in naturally
without effort. We can chew food.
When we had cavities, the dentist
fixed them for us. There are
so many things to be thankful for.

We have bones that support our body every day. Be thankful for bones too.

(60)

Be thankful for having a brain

that continues to work

without a day's rest.

We have ears and can hear

what other people say.

How mysterious yet marvelous

this system is.

(62)

We are given sight and sound.

Oh, how much richer life

has become.

We can breathe and talk

thanks to our throat and lungs.

What a blessing!

(64)

How happy we are to have hands

and fingers to write or

to even type on a keyboard.

We can digest what we eat and

absorb the nutrition thanks to

our stomachs and intestines.

What a joy it is!

(66)

People die if they cannot urinate.

Have you ever thanked organs

such as your kidneys?

Our life continues thanks to

the anus functioning every day.

Genitals cause worries

but also create happiness.

They have even contributed to

the creation of human history.

Feet are not just for walking.

Some people can even draw

pictures with their toes.

Strengthening your legs leads

you to accomplish much work.

Even Shakyamuni Buddha

continued his journey of

missionary work on foot.

(71)

Thanks to our brain and our limbs, we were blessed with so many possibilities in our life.

Thanks to language classes,

our way of life is very different

from how animals live.

(73)

Thanks to arithmetic,

we can now do business;

thanks to mathematics,

we can now create

buildings and vehicles.

Thanks to food and medicine,

the age of longevity has arrived.

(75)

Thanks to studying English,

we can now travel abroad

and trade.

Thanks to studying science,

we can now understand about

plants, living creatures, and even

the mysteries of the universe.

Thanks to social studies,

we learned about people's way of

life and how to make this world

a better place to live in.

Thanks to fine arts,

we could make beauty

a part of our happiness.

(79)

Thanks to music, we could create another world of happiness.

(80)

Ah, how wonderful it is

to be able to read novels and

watch movies.

How wonderful it is to have

the chance to get married,

or to have been married and

wish for the happiness of

your ex even after divorce.

If you don't have children, you

have the happiness of being free.

If you have children, you have

hope for the future.

It is a blessing to have family

who gives their opinions and

relatives who care about

your reputation.

Friendships have nurtured you
and friends have helped you grow.

The experience of being poor

made you appreciate the

true value of wealth.

The joy of getting your paycheck
in hand; the joy of having
enough money to live on.

The pain of job hunting;

the joy of getting the job.

88

The joy of knowing

you have a talent.

The joy of becoming a husband,

wife, father, or mother.

The joy of awakening to
"desiring little and
knowing contentment."

The joy of awakening to

your mission and your calling.

The joy of knowing there is
an unseen world waiting for us
after leaving this world.

93

The joy of having things that
you are still able to do; the joy of
being needed by others.

The joy of being able to love others. The joy of being able to make peace with someone you hated.

(95)

The joy of understanding
that you won't become a lost
spirit after death.

Remember the Pauper's candle:

the joy of being able to give

gratitude to God and Buddha

even if poor.

$$\textcircled{97}$$

The joy of being able to practice
the "Exploration of Right Mind"
every day.

The happiness of understanding

that self-reflection also brings

you closer to God.

99

The peace that comes from
knowing that both heaven and
hell exist under Buddha's Truth.

Devoting yourself to the
teachings of the Real Buddha;
this is the joy deeply rooted in
human souls.

Afterword and Commentary

I feel that many people are seeking a book that they can take their time and read repeatedly when suffering from an illness at home or in the hospital. To answer their needs, I have written this book.

Times of illness are also times for you to recall things you have overlooked in everyday life. It is also when you realize the abundance of happiness that surrounds you.

The phrases in this book were inspired by the spirits of Edgar Cayce and Yamrozay, one of the highest-ranked angels (Seraphim).

What's more, please note that when writing this book, I repeatedly listened to the songs (CDs) from the Happy Science movie series *Heart to Heart*, such as *Living in the Age of Miracles* and *Life Is Beautiful*. I believe that these songs will also help you recover from illness.

> *Ryuho Okawa*
> *Master & CEO of Happy Science Group*
> *January 17, 2023*

ABOUT THE AUTHOR

Founder and CEO of Happy Science Group.

Ryuho Okawa was born on July 7th 1956, in Tokushima, Japan. After graduating from the University of Tokyo with a law degree, he joined a Tokyo-based trading house. While working at its New York headquarters, he studied international finance at the Graduate Center of the City University of New York. In 1981, he attained Great Enlightenment and became aware that he is El Cantare with a mission to bring salvation to all humankind.

In 1986, he established Happy Science. It now has members in 168 countries across the world, with more than 700 branches and temples as well as 10,000 missionary houses around the world.

He has given over 3,500 lectures (of which more than 150 are in English) and published over 3,100 books (of which more than 600 are Spiritual Interview Series), and many are translated into 41 languages. Along with *The Laws of the Sun* and *The Laws of Hell*, many of the books have become best sellers or million sellers. To date, Happy Science has produced 27 movies under the supervision of Okawa. He has given the original story and concept and is also the Executive Producer. He has also composed music and written lyrics of over 450 pieces.

Moreover, he is the Founder of Happy Science University and Happy Science Academy (Junior and Senior High School), Founder and President of the Happiness Realization Party, Founder and Honorary Headmaster of Happy Science Institute of Government and Management, Founder of IRH Press Co., Ltd., and the Chairperson of NEW STAR PRODUCTION Co., Ltd. and ARI Production Co., Ltd.

BOOKS BY RYUHO OKAWA

Words of Wisdom Series

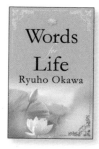

Words for Life

Paperback • 136 pages • $15.95
ISBN: 979-8-88727-089-7 (Mar. 16, 2023)

Ryuho Okawa has written over 3,100 books on various topics. To help readers find the teachings that are beneficial for them out of the extensive teachings, the author has written 100 phrases and put them together in this book. Inside you will find words of wisdom that will help you improve your mindset and lead you to live a meaningful and happy life.

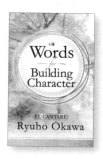

Words for Building Character

Paperback • 140 pages • $15.95
ISBN: 979-8-88737-091-0 (Jun. 21, 2023)

As you read this book, you will discover the wisdom to build a noble character through various life experiences. When your life comes to an end, what you can bring with you to the other world is, in Buddhism terms, enlightenment, and in other words, it is the character that you build in this lifetime. If you can read, relish, and truly understand the meaning of these religious phrases, you will be able to attain happiness that transcends this world and the next.

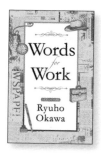

Words for Work

Paperback • 140 pages • $15.95
ISBN: 979-8-88737-090-3 (Jul. 20, 2023)

Through his personal experiences at work and receiving inspiration from God and the angels in the heavenly world, Master Okawa has created these phrases regarding philosophies and practical wisdom about work. Have this book on your desk and it will be of great use to you throughout your career. Every day you can contemplate and gain tips on how to better your work as well as deepen your insight into company management.

Healing Books

Healing from Within

Life-Changing Keys to Calm, Spiritual, and Healthy Living

Paperback • 208 pages • $15.95
ISBN:978-1-942125-18-1 (Jun. 30, 2017)

None of us wants to become sick, but why is it that we can't avoid illness in life? Is there a meaning behind illness? In this book, author Ryuho Okawa reveals the true causes and remedies for various illnesses that modern medicine doesn't know how to heal. Building a happier and healthier life starts with believing in the power of our mind and understanding the relationship between mind and body.

Worry-Free Living

Let Go of Stress and Live in Peace and Happiness

Hardcover • 192 pages • $16.95
ISBN: 978-1-942125-51-8 (May 15, 2019)

The wisdom Ryuho Okawa shares in this book about facing problems in human relationships, financial hardships, and other life's stresses will help you change how you look at and approach life's worries and problems for the better. Let this book be your guide to finding precious meaning in all your life's problems, gaining inner growth and practicing inner happiness and spiritual growth.

Healing Power

The True Mechanism of Mind and Illness

Paperback • 190 pages • $14.95
ISBN: 979-8-88737-048-4 (Feb. 18, 2016)

This book describes the relationship between the mind and illness, and provides you with hints to restore your mental and physical health. By reading this book, you can find tips on how to heal your body from illnesses such as cancer, heart disease, allergy, skin disease, dementia, psychiatric disorder, and atopy. You will gain the miraculous power of healing.

El Cantare Trilogy

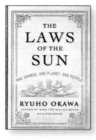

The Laws of the Sun

One Source, One Planet, One People

Paperback • 288 pages • $15.95
ISBN: 978-1-942125-43-3 (Apr. 20, 2021)

Imagine if you could ask God why he created this world and what spiritual laws he used to shape us—and everything around us. Ryuho Okawa outlines these laws of the universe and provides a road map for living one's life with greater purpose and meaning. This powerful book shows the way to realize true happiness—a happiness that continues from this world through the other.

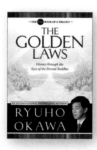

The Golden Laws

History through the Eyes of the Eternal Buddha

E-book • 204 pages • $13.99
ISBN: 978-1-941779-82-8 (Sep. 24, 2015)

Throughout history, Great Guiding Spirits of Light have been present on Earth in both the East and the West at crucial points in human history to further our spiritual development. *The Golden Laws* reveals how Divine Plan has been unfolding on Earth, and outlines 5,000 years of the secret history of humankind.

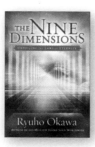

The Nine Dimensions

Unveiling the Laws of Eternity

Paperback • 168 pages • $15.95
ISBN: 978-0-982698-56-3 (Feb. 16, 2012)

This book is a window into the mind of our loving God. When the religions and cultures of the world discover the truth of their common spiritual origin, they will be inspired to accept their differences, come together under faith in God, and build an era of harmony and peaceful progress on Earth.

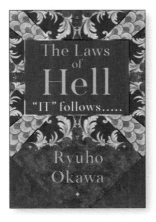

The Laws of Hell

"IT" follows.....

Paperback • 264 pages • $17.95
ISBN: 978-1-958655-04-7 (May 1, 2023)

Whether you believe it or not, the Spirit World and hell do exist. Currently, the Earth's population has exceeded 8 billion, and unfortunately, 1 in 2 people are falling to hell.

This book is a must-read at a time like this since more and more people are unknowingly heading to hell; the truth is, new areas of hell are being created, such as 'internet hell' and 'hell on earth.' Also, due to the widespread materialism, there is a sharp rise in the earthbound spirits wandering around Earth because they have no clue about the Spirit World.

To stop hell from spreading and to save the souls of all human beings, Ryuho Okawa has compiled vital teachings in this book. This publication marks his 3,100th book and is the one and only comprehensive Truth about the modern hell.

New Books

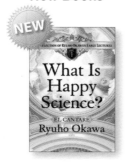

What Is Happy Science?
Best Selection of Ryuho Okawa's Early Lectures (Volume 1)

Paperback • 256 pages • $17.95
ISBN: 978-1-942125-99-0 (Aug. 25, 2023)

The Best Selection series is a collection of Ryuho Okawa's passionate lectures during the ages of 32 to 33 that reveal the mission and goal of Happy Science. This book contains the eternal Truth, including the meaning of life, the secret of the mind, the true meaning of love, the mystery of the universe, and how to end hatred and world conflicts.

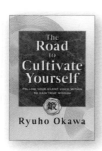

The Road to Cultivate Yourself
Follow Your Silent Voice Within to Gain True Wisdom

Paperback • 256 pages • $17.95
ISBN: 978-1-958655-05-4 (Jun. 22, 2023)

What is the ideal way of living when chaos and destruction are accelerated?

This book offers unchanging Truth in the ever-changing world, such as the secrets to become more aware about the spiritual self and how to increase intellectual productivity amidst the rapid changes of the modern age. It is packed with Ryuho Okawa's crystallized wisdom of life.

The Challenge of Enlightenment
Now, Here, the New Dharma Wheel Turns

Paperback • 380 pages • $17.95
ISBN: 978-1-942125-92-1 (Dec. 20, 2022)

Buddha's teachings, a reflection of his eternal wisdom, are like a bamboo pole used to change the course of your boat in the rapid stream of the great river called life. By reading this book, your mind becomes clearer, learns to savor inner peace, and it will empower you to make profound life improvements.

Bestselling Buddhist Titles

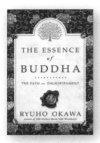

The Essence of Buddha

The Path to Enlightenment

Paperback • 208 pages • $14.95
ISBN: 978-1-942125-06-8 (Oct.1, 2016)

The essence of Shakyamuni Buddha's original teachings of the mind are explained in simple language: how to attain inner happiness, the wisdom to conquer ego, and the path to enlightenment for people in the contemporary era. It is a way of life that anyone can practice to achieve lifelong self-growth.

The Challenge of the Mind

An Essential Guide to Buddha's Teachings: Zen, Karma and Enlightenment

Paperback • 208 pages • $16.95
ISBN: 978-1-942125-45-7 (Nov. 15, 2018)

In this book, Ryuho Okawa explains essential Buddhist tenets and how to put them into practice. Enlightenment is not just an abstract idea but one that everyone can experience to some extent. Okawa offers a solid basis of reason and intellectual understanding to Buddhist concepts. By applying these basic principles to our lives, we can direct our minds to higher ideals and create a bright future for ourselves and others.

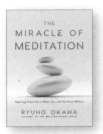

The Miracle of Meditation

Opening Your Life to Peace, Joy, and the Power Within

Paperback • 207 pages • $15.95
ISBN: 978-1-942125-09-9 (Nov. 1, 2016)

This book introduces various types of meditation, including calming meditation, purposeful meditation, reading meditation, reflective meditation, and meditation to communicate with heaven. Through reading and practicing meditation in this book, we can experience the miracle of meditation, which is to start living a life of peace, happiness, and success.

The Ten Principles from El Cantare Volume I
Ryuho Okawa's First Lectures on His Basic Teachings

The Ten Principles from El Cantare Volume II
Ryuho Okawa's First Lectures on His Wish to Save the World

The True Eightfold Path
Guideposts for Self-innovation

The Laws of Happiness
Love, Wisdom, Self-Reflection and Progress

The Rebirth of Buddha
My Eternal Disciples, Hear My Words

The Starting Point of Happiness
An Inspiring Guide to Positive Living with
Faith, Love, and Courage

The Laws of Hope
The Light is Here

The Power of Basics
Introduction to Modern Zen Life
of Calm, Spirituality and Success

The Strong Mind
The Art of Building the Inner Strength to
Overcome Life's Difficulties

For a complete list of books, visit okawabooks.com

MUSIC BY RYUHO OKAWA

The following are El Cantare Ryuho Okawa Original Songs mentioned in the Afterword and Commentary. These songs are from the "Heart to Heart" series (documentary film).

Heart to Heart
The theme song of the movie "Heart to Heart"

Life Is Beautiful
The theme song of the movie "Life Is Beautiful"

Living in the Age of Miracles
The theme song of the movie
"Living in the Age of Miracles"

Awakening
The insert song of the movie
"Living in the Age of Miracles"

From Sadness To Delight
The feature song of the movie "Living in the Age of Miracles"

Listen now today!

 Spotify | iTunes | Amazon

CD available at Shopify (irhpress.com),
and Happy Science locations worldwide

WHO IS EL CANTARE?

El Cantare means "the Light of the Earth." He is the Supreme God of the Earth who has been guiding humankind since the beginning of Genesis, and He is the Creator of the universe. He is whom Jesus called Father and Muhammad called Allah, and is *Ame-no-Mioya-Gami*, Japanese Father God. Different parts of El Cantare's core consciousness have descended to Earth in the past, once as Alpha and another as Elohim. His branch spirits, such as Shakyamuni Buddha and Hermes, have descended to Earth many times and helped to flourish many civilizations. To unite various religions and to integrate various fields of study in order to build a new civilization on Earth, a part of the core consciousness has descended to Earth as Master Ryuho Okawa.

Alpha is a part of the core consciousness of El Cantare who descended to Earth around 330 million years ago. Alpha preached Earth's Truths to harmonize and unify Earth-born humans and space people who came from other planets.

Elohim is a part of the core consciousness of El Cantare who descended to Earth around 150 million years ago. He gave wisdom, mainly on the differences of light and darkness, good and evil.

Ame-no-Mioya-Gami (Japanese Father God) is the Creator God and the Father God who appears in the ancient literature, *Hotsuma Tsutae*. It is believed that He descended on the foothills of Mt. Fuji about 30,000 years ago and built the Fuji dynasty, which is the root of the Japanese civilization. With justice as the central pillar, Ame-no-Mioya-Gami's teachings spread to ancient civilizations of other countries in the world.

Shakyamuni Buddha was born as a prince into the Shakya Clan in India around 2,600 years ago. When he was 29 years old, he renounced the world and sought enlightenment. He later attained Great Enlightenment and founded Buddhism.

Hermes is one of the 12 Olympian gods in Greek mythology, but the spiritual Truth is that he taught the teachings of love and progress around 4,300 years ago that became the origin of the current Western civilization. He is a hero that truly existed.

Ophealis was born in Greece around 6,500 years ago and was the leader who took an expedition to as far as Egypt. He is the God of miracles, prosperity, and arts, and is known as Osiris in the Egyptian mythology.

Rient Arl Croud was born as a king of the ancient Incan Empire around 7,000 years ago and taught about the mysteries of the mind. In the heavenly world, he is responsible for the interactions that take place between various planets.

Thoth was an almighty leader who built the golden age of the Atlantic civilization around 12,000 years ago. In the Egyptian mythology, he is known as God Thoth.

Ra Mu was a leader who built the golden age of the civilization of Mu around 17,000 years ago. As a religious leader and a politician, he ruled by uniting religion and politics.

ABOUT HAPPY SCIENCE

Happy Science is a religious group founded on the faith in El Cantare who is the God of the Earth, and the Creator of the universe. The essence of human beings is the soul that was created by God, and we all are children of God. God is our true parent, so in our souls we have a fundamental desire to "believe in God, love God, and get closer to God." And, we can get closer to God by living with God's Will as our own. In Happy Science, we call this the "Exploration of Right Mind." More specifically, it means to practice the Fourfold Path, which consists of "Love, Wisdom, Self-Reflection, and Progress."

Love: Love means "love that gives," or mercy. God hopes for the happiness of all people. Therefore, living with God's Will as our own means to start by practicing "love that gives."

Wisdom: By studying and putting spiritual knowledge into practice, you can cultivate wisdom and become better at resolving problems in life.

Self-Reflection: Once you learn the heart of God and the difference between His mind and yours, you should strive to bring your own mind closer to the mind of God—that process is called self-reflection. Self-reflection also includes meditation and prayer.

Progress: Since God hopes for the happiness of all people, you should also make progress in your love, and make an effort to realize utopia in which everyone in your society, country, and eventually all humankind can become happy.

As we practice this Fourfold Path, our souls will advance toward God step by step. That is when we can attain real happiness— our souls' desire to get closer to God comes true.

In Happy Science, we conduct activities to make ourselves happy through belief in Lord El Cantare, and to spread this faith to the world and bring happiness to all. We welcome you to join our activities!

We hold events and activities to help you practice the Fourfold Path at our branches, temples, missionary centers and missionary houses

Love: We hold various volunteering activities. Our members conduct missionary work together as the greatest practice of love.

Wisdom: We offer our comprehensive books collection, many of which are available online and at Happy Science locations. In addition, we give out numerous opportunities such as seminars or book clubs to learn the Truth.

Self-Reflection: We offer opportunities to polish your mind through self-reflection, meditation, and prayer. There are many cases in which members have experienced improvement in their human relationships by changing their own minds.

Progress: We also offer seminars to enhance your power of influence. Because it is also important to do well at work to make society better, we hold seminars to improve your work and management skills.

HAPPY SCIENCE'S ENGLISH SUTRA

"The True Words Spoken By Buddha"

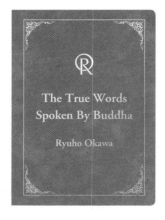

The True Words Spoken By Buddha is an English sutra given directly from the spirit of Shakyamuni Buddha, who is a part of Master Ryuho Okawa's subconscious. The words in this sutra are not of a mere human being but are the words of God or Buddha sent directly from the ninth dimension, which is the highest realm of the Earth's Spirit World.

The True Words Spoken By Buddha is an essential sutra for us to connect and live with God or Buddha's Will as our own.

MEMBERSHIPS

MEMBERSHIP

If you would like to know more about Happy Science, please consider becoming a member. Those who pledge to believe in Lord El Cantare and wish to learn more can join us.

When you become a member, you will receive the following sutra books: *The True Words Spoken By Buddha*, *Prayer to the Lord* and *Prayer to Guardian and Guiding Spirits*.

DEVOTEE MEMBER

If you would like to learn the teachings of Happy Science and walk the path of faith, become a Devotee member who pledges devotion to the Three Treasures, which are Buddha, Dharma, and Sangha. Buddha refers to Lord El Cantare, Master Ryuho Okawa. Dharma refers to Master Ryuho Okawa's teachings. Sangha refers to Happy Science. Devoting to the Three Treasures will let your Buddha-nature shine, and you will enter the path to attain true freedom of the mind.

Becoming a devotee means you become Buddha's disciple. You will discipline your mind and act to bring happiness to society.

✉ EMAIL or ☎ PHONE CALL

Please see the contact information page.

☎ ONLINE member.happy-science.org/signup/ 🔍

CONTACT INFORMATION

Happy Science is a worldwide organization with branches and temples around the globe. For a comprehensive list, visit the worldwide directory at happy-science.org. The following are some of our main Happy Science locations:

UNITED STATES AND CANADA

New York
79 Franklin St., New York, NY 10013, USA
Phone: 1-212-343-7972
Fax: 1-212-343-7973
Email: ny@happy-science.org
Website: happyscience-usa.org

New Jersey
66 Hudson St., #2R, Hoboken, NJ 07030, USA
Phone: 1-201-313-0127
Email: nj@happy-science.org
Website: happyscience-usa.org

Chicago
2300 Barrington Rd., Suite #400,
Hoffman Estates, IL 60169, USA
Phone: 1-630-937-3077
Email: chicago@happy-science.org
Website: happyscience-usa.org

Florida
5208 8th St., Zephyrhills, FL 33542, USA
Phone: 1-813-715-0000
Fax: 1-813-715-0010
Email: florida@happy-science.org
Website: happyscience-usa.org

Atlanta
1874 Piedmont Ave., NE Suite 360-C
Atlanta, GA 30324, USA
Phone: 1-404-892-7770
Email: atlanta@happy-science.org
Website: happyscience-usa.org

San Francisco
525 Clinton St. Redwood City, CA 94062, USA
Phone & Fax: 1-650-363-2777
Email: sf@happy-science.org
Website: happyscience-usa.org

Los Angeles
1590 E. Del Mar Blvd., Pasadena, CA 91106, USA
Phone: 1-626-395-7775
Fax: 1-626-395-7776
Email: la@happy-science.org
Website: happyscience-usa.org

Orange County
16541 Gothard St. Suite 104 Huntington
Beach, CA 92647
Phone: 1-714-659-1501
Email: oc@happy-science.org
Website: happyscience-usa.org

San Diego
7841 Balboa Ave. Suite #202 San Diego,
CA 92111, USA
Phone: 1-626-395-7775
Fax: 1-626-395-7776
E-mail: sandiego@happy-science.org
Website: happyscience-usa.org

Hawaii
Phone: 1-808-591-9772
Fax: 1-808-591-9776
Email: hi@happy-science.org
Website: happyscience-usa.org

Kauai
3343 Kanakolu Street, Suite 5 Lihue,
HI 96766, USA
Phone: 1-808-822-7007
Fax: 1-808-822-6007
Email: kauai-hi@happy-science.org
Website: happyscience-usa.org

Toronto
845 The Queensway
Etobicoke, ON M8Z 1N6, Canada
Phone: 1-416-901-3747
Email: toronto@happy-science.org
Website: happy-science.ca

INTERNATIONAL

Tokyo
1-6-7 Togoshi, Shinagawa,
Tokyo, 142-0041, Japan
Phone: 81-3-6384-5770
Fax: 81-3-6384-5776
Email: tokyo@happy-science.org
Website: happy-science.org

London
3 Margaret St.
London, W1W 8RE United Kingdom
Phone: 44-20-7323-9255
Fax: 44-20-7323-9344
Email: eu@happy-science.org
Website: www.happyscience-uk.org

Sydney
516 Pacific Highway, Lane Cove North,
2066 NSW, Australia
Phone: 61-2-9411-2877
Fax: 61-2-9411-2822
Email: sydney@happy-science.org

Sao Paulo
Rua. Domingos de Morais 1154, Vila Mariana,
Sao Paulo SP CEP 04010-100, Brazil
Phone: 55-11-5088-3800
Email: sp@happy-science.org
Website: happyscience.com.br

Jundiai
Rua Congo, 447, Jd. Bonfiglioli
Jundiai-CEP, 13207-340, Brazil
Phone: 55-11-4587-5952
Email: jundiai@happy-science.org

Vancouver
#201-2607 East 49th Avenue,
Vancouver, BC, V5S 1J9, Canada
Phone: 1-604-437-7735
Fax: 1-604-437-7764
Email: vancouver@happy-science.org
Website: happy-science.ca

Seoul
74, Sadang-ro 27-gil, Dongjak-gu, Seoul, Korea
Phone: 82-2-3478-8777
Fax: 82-2-3478-9777
Email: korea@happy-science.org

Taipei
No. 89, Lane 155, Dunhua N. Road,
Songshan District, Taipei City 105, Taiwan
Phone: 886-2-2719-9377
Fax: 886-2-2719-5570
Email: taiwan@happy-science.org

Taichung
No. 146, Minzu Rd., Central Dist.,
Taichung City 400001, Taiwan (R.O.C.)
Phone: 886-4-22233777
Email: taichung@happy-science.org

Kuala Lumpur
No 22A, Block 2, Jalil Link Jalan Jalil Jaya 2,
Bukit Jalil 57000,
Kuala Lumpur, Malaysia
Phone: 60-3-8998-7877
Fax: 60-3-8998-7977
Email: malaysia@happy-science.org
Website: happyscience.org.my

Kathmandu
Kathmandu Metropolitan City, Ward No. 15,
Ring Road, Kimdol, Sitapaila Kathmandu, Nepal
Phone: 977-1-537-2931
Email: nepal@happy-science.org

Kampala
Plot 877 Rubaga Road, Kampala
P.O. Box 34130 Kampala, UGANDA
Email: uganda@happy-science.org

ABOUT IRH PRESS USA

IRH Press USA Inc. was founded in 2013 as an affiliated firm of IRH Press Co., Ltd., based in New York. The press exclusively publishes comprehensive titles by Ryuho Okawa, an international bestselling author who has written more than 3,100 titles on Self-Improvement, Spiritual Truth, Religious Truth and more, with 100 million copies sold worldwide. For more information, visit okawabooks.com.

Follow us on:

f Facebook: Okawa Books   **◯** Instagram: OkawaBooks

▶ Youtube: Okawa Books   **🐦** Twitter: Okawa Books

𝓟 Pinterest: Okawa Books   **g** Goodreads: Ryuho Okawa

——— **NEWSLETTER** ———

To receive book related news, promotions and events, please subscribe to our newsletter below.

∞ irhpress.com/pages/subscribe

——— **AUDIO / VISUAL MEDIA** ———

YOUTUBE   PODCAST

Introduction of Ryuho Okawa's titles; topics ranging from self-help, current affairs, spirituality, religion, and the universe.